Flowers Are CALLING

Words by Rita Gray

Pictures by
Kenard Pak

Clarion Books
An Imprint of HarperCollins*Publishers*
Boston   New York

Flowers are calling a little black bear.

No, not a bear! He doesn't care.

They're calling a butterfly
to dip from the air.

Flowers are calling a wet green frog.
No, not a frog! She likes her soggy bog.

They're calling a bumblebee
to look near their log.

Flowers are calling a porcupine.

No, not a porcupine! She wouldn't take the time.

They're calling a hummingbird
to sip at their vine.

Queen Anne's Lace

Butterflies like a landing pad
when they drink nectar.

Monkshood

Bumblebees are hefty enough to push deep inside a monkshood flower, where nectar is stored.

Trumpet Honeysuckle

Hummingbirds use their long tongues to reach the nectar hidden in deep tubular flowers, and hover as they drink.

Flowers are calling a loud blue jay.
No, not a jay! He wouldn't stay.

They're calling a honeybee
to fly their way.

Flowers are calling a little moose.

No, not a moose! What would be the use?

They're calling a beetle
to eat their pollen loose.

Flowers are calling a rabbit to stop.

No, not a rabbit! It's not their habit to call a rabbit.

He might grab it!

They're calling a bee fly
to visit their spot.

Apple Tree Blossom

Honeybees help make many of the fruits, nuts, and vegetables
we eat by pollinating fruit tree blossoms such as the apple tree.
There are also thousands of varieties of wild bees that help to
make many of the foods we eat.

Magnolia

Beetles have been visiting flowers for
more than 100 million years.

Violet

Bee flies look like bumblebees but have two wings instead of four.
Like hummingbirds, they are able to hover their furry bodies in
the air as they drink nectar.

Flowers are calling a small brown snake.
No, not a snake, for goodness' sake!

They're calling a pollen wasp
with nectar to take.

Flowers are calling a fat raccoon.
No, not a raccoon! He doesn't care for
white bloom or sweet perfume.

They're calling a moth,
in the light of the moon.

Flowers are calling a desert deer.
No, not a deer! He can't even get near.

They're calling a nectar bat
to flap over here.

Blowout Beard Tongue

Pollen wasps, like bees, make loaves of nectar
and pollen to feed their young.

Cardon Cactus

Lesser long-nosed bats have long tongues that can reach the nectar deep inside the bell-shaped flowers of the cardon cactus. These cactus flowers unfurl for just one short night.

Moonflower and Carolina Sphinx Moth

Sphinx moths are expert fliers with very long tongues. Like cardon cactus, the blooms of moonflowers open for just one night and depend on the nighttime visits of moths for pollination.

Flowers are calling a busy wren.

No, not a wren! He's already seen them.

They're calling some children
to look again.

Look at a flower—what do you see?

Color

Flowers that have daytime visitors tend to have bright colors so they can be easily found among all the green foliage. Flowers with nighttime visitors tend to be pale with a very sweet smell, making them easier to locate in the dark. Many insects can't see the color red and are instead drawn to yellows and blues.

Pattern

Many flowers use designs to help the pollinator find nectar right away. These designs are called nectar guides. How is the middle of your flower different from its outer part? Would these differences help a pollinator find nectar?

Shape

The shape of a flower can tell you who might come to visit. Hummingbirds can reach deep inside long, thin flowers, but honeybees have rather short tongues. They need their nectar served in shallow golden bowls, like those of the apple blossom. Bumblebees are rather heavy and need strong flowers that can hold their heft. Is your flower a tight cluster of many small blossoms, such as Queen Anne's lace or dandelion? Then it will be good for all those insects that like a sturdy perch.

Smell

Does your flower smell sweet or musky? Does it have any smell at all? Bees like sweet smells, and beetles like fruity, spicy scents. Night-active moths love flowers as fragrant as perfume. Nectar bats like musky smells, and some flies like rotten smells. Birds and butterflies use their eyes to find flowers instead of their sense of smell.

Time of Opening

Does your flower open in the daytime or the nighttime? If it is a night bloomer, it is calling to a night moth or nectar bat. Day bloomers are calling to birds and insects who find food in the sunshine.

Would You Believe!

Flowers need pollinators to flourish, and pollinators need flowers for nourishment. A pollinator is any animal or insect that helps a flower to trade pollen with another flower like itself. Most flowers need to trade pollen with each other so they can make seeds. These seeds will then grow into new plants. Here are some fascinating ways flowers call to their special pollinators:

Many insects and birds see in ultraviolet light. This allows them to see nectar guides that are invisible to us. A flower that appears to us as one solid color can actually have a prominent two-toned bull's-eye at its center. This sends a loud and clear message: *Drink here!*

Some early-spring flowers create their own heat to give visiting insects a toasty room for the night. This ability to generate heat is called thermogenesis. This warmth also helps spread a flower's scent.

Some flowers of coffee, orange, and grapefruit plants offer bees a shot of caffeine with their nectar. The bees like the caffeine and return to the blossoms for refills. The caffeine helps the bees to remember where they found it.

Flowers make their own electrical buzz that bees understand. This buzz can tell a bee how much nectar a flower has. In this way flowers signal to bees which flowers offer a full slurp of nectar.

Bees, birds, butterflies, moths, bats, and other pollinators are some of the most important creatures on earth. When they drink the nectar of flowers and/or eat flower pollen, they help plants to make new flowers. Some of these flowers become the fruits, nuts, and vegetables we eat every day. But pollinators are in trouble, and we can help. Perfectly manicured green lawns that use toxic herbicides and pesticides offer nothing to pollinators. What they need instead are long grasses, with an assortment of native species flowers. Ideally, the flowers will be lots of different colors and shapes, and bloom throughout the growing season. Even a few flowerpots or a window box can make a difference. And don't forget to include a fresh water source for your precious pollinators.

To find out how to attract pollinators in your specific area, enter your zipcode at
pollinator.org/guides.htm.

For Rinaldo and our wildflowers —R.G.
To my patient wife, Jenn —K.P.

Special thanks to Beatriz Moisset for her devotion to pollinators
and for her help in insuring the accuracy of this book.

clarionbooks.com

The text of this book is set in Cronos Pro and Amorie.
The art is watercolor and digital media.

Library of Congress Cataloging-in-Publication Data is on file.

ISBN 978-0-544-34012-1

Manufactured in Vietnam
23 SCP 15 14 13 12 11 10